DISCIPLE

BECOMING DISCIPLES THROUGH BIBLE STUDY

Personal Study Guide

Writers of
DISCIPLE: BECOMING DISCIPLES THROUGH BIBLE STUDY

Richard Byrd Wilke
Julia Kitchens Wilke

Personal Study Guide
Adapted by Marvin Cropsey

12 13 14 15 15 16 17 18 19 20—10 9 8 7 6 5 4 3 2

CONTENTS

DISCIPLE

BEFORE YOU START

HOW DO I STUDY DISCIPLE BY MYSELF?

In March 1986, a small group of people gathered in Flower Mound, Texas, to talk about the need for a new comprehensive Bible study that would do more than teach the facts about our Scriptures. They wanted a study that would help people place themselves within the narrative of the Scriptures, develop a conversation with the Scriptures, and find their personal meaning for life in the Scriptures. Beyond that, they wanted a Bible study that would help persons grow in faith as they lived out a life of discipleship among the people of God.

DISCIPLE Bible Study was the result of those conversations. The plan called for a small group of people (modeled after Jesus Christ's twelve disciples) to spend 34 weeks intensively studying the entire 66 books of the Bible, with daily readings from the Bible, prayer, lessons in a Study Manual, and a weekly gathering for 2½ hours. Church governing boards would have to approve the program, teachers would have to be specially trained, and students would pledge their commitment.

You may first have learned about DISCIPLE Bible Study many years ago. Perhaps at that time, you were drawn to this new study but didn't have access to a group. Or you didn't have the required time every day, or you thought that you had to already know Scriptures to be involved. So you didn't join a study. Now you have picked up this book that indicates that DISCIPLE Bible Study is available for individual study. Perhaps your earlier interest is revived. Perhaps the reasons you didn't previously begin DISCIPLE remain true.

Alternatively, perhaps you are just now discovering DISCIPLE Bible Study. But maybe group study seems impossible for you at this time, or maybe the time you have to study is so limited that you must pick it up whenever and wherever you can.

In either case, this DISCIPLE *Personal Study Guide* is for you.

Please note that this Personal Study Guide is not a replacement for the DISCIPLE Study Manual. It is a guide for use of the Study Manual. Supplemental videos that feature leading biblical scholars in 10- to 15-minute sessions on DVD are also available for purchase from Cokesbury. Or you might choose to borrow them from your local church. Audio versions are available for download from Cokesbury.com.

You may be wondering: If discipleship is about modeling the life of Christ in community, how can I study discipleship alone in my room? Our answer: It's true that you will spend time studying alone. In fact, several million people who have used DISCIPLE Bible Study during the last twenty years did ninety percent of their study alone in their room during the week. Unlike them, however, you will not gather for group study. This you will do by yourself. But this guide gives you a plan to do that and, more important, tells you how to reach beyond yourself to interact with the people who populate your life and your world. The guide will serve as a door from your personal study to the world beyond, where you will practice what you have learned.

Some features of this book are unchanged from the original DISCIPLE course. You will still use the Study Manual to guide your daily Bible readings. You will decide how to schedule each day's session. At the conclusion of each week's study, you will have an individual time of review and contemplation. You will still reflect on the theme word, theme verse, and "Our Human Condition"; and you will pray the opening prayer. You will still consider the "Marks of Discipleship" and how they relate to you. And you will close by praying for those persons who are a part of your life.

Other features of this book are different from the original DISCIPLE course. One significant difference is that the week-ending meeting with a group of fellow Christians will be replaced by a week-ending summary session—time alone to review; contemplate; plan for your coming week; and, if you so choose, view the DVD or listen to the audio recording. The length of time you spend in this summary session is entirely up to you, but you should allow enough time to be thoughtful and thorough. In this Personal Study Guide, you will find plans for each weekly summary session. (See Summary Sessions, pages 19–89.)

Since you have undertaken this comprehensive study alone, you should consider strengthening your commitment to community by telling at least two faith friends about your study. Occasionally, in the pages of this guide, you will be asked to write to or phone a faith friend to share something specific. At the conclusion of your study, you will have the opportunity to include these friends in your celebration.

You will also find in this guide many suggestions for training yourself to study effectively. These suggestions include principles of Bible study, how to use each section of the guide, how to form good questions during your study, and how to take notes and mark your Bible.

You will be studying alone, but you do not live outside society. You can practice the Christian lifestyle with those you talk to on the phone, with those you encounter at work and in church, with those in the cars before and after you on the road. Your community is truly all around you.

How will you express your belief in Jesus Christ through the way you live? To answer that question, you are about to undertake the greatest study of your life, a study that may begin with DISCIPLE but will, by the grace of God, extend through all the days of your life.

PUT THE STUDY MANUAL TO WORK

The DISCIPLE Study Manual is the most important tool in DISCIPLE Bible Study. Each part of the Study Manual has a specific function both in daily preparation and in your weekly summary session.

THEME WORD

The theme word gives a clue to the subject of the lesson and the Scripture being studied in the lesson. The following tips may help you as you study:

— Display the word as you study.

— Consider memorizing the theme word along with the lesson title to help you recall the sequence and content of the biblical story.

THEME VERSE

The theme verse (or verses) expresses the focus of the lesson and might be recited from memory or read during your opening moment of devotion.

TITLE

The title is descriptive of events or content; and taken altogether, the titles summarize the biblical story from Creation to the Revelation.

OUR HUMAN CONDITION

"Our Human Condition" is a statement of who we are. The "Marks of Discipleship" are statements of whom we are committing ourselves to become; and as such, they suggest a resolution to "Our Human Condition." Restating "Our Human Condition" in terms of your own experience will give you a genuine opportunity to turn what could be an academic Bible study into a life-changing adventure.

ASSIGNMENT

Scripture is central to DISCIPLE, and the gaining and maintaining of the discipline of daily reading and study of Scripture are essential to the process of becoming disciples.

The "Assignment" section indicates when to read the week's Scripture and when to read the Study Manual and write the responses called for.

— Practice daily note-taking along with daily Scripture reading. The second page of each lesson in the Study Manual provides space. The main purpose for taking notes is to have a personal record of information gleaned from Scripture and of insights and questions about the Scripture. This will be particularly helpful when you enjoy your summary session at the end of the week of study.

— Share with someone who is important to you in your faith journey that you are about to undertake a major Bible study, and ask him or her to pray for your efforts.

— Be diligent in marking your Bible as you read. (See "Marking Your Bible," on page 13.)

— In your weekly summary session. make use of all of the work you have done during the week.

PRAYER

The prayer psalm printed in this guide is a starting point for personal prayer.

— Jot down concerns you want to pray about during the week, and add concerns as they arise during your daily study of Scripture.

— Sending a note occasionally to those for whom you are praying can add dimension and power to your Bible study. Doing so will be part of your discipleship. From time to time, converse with the spiritual friend you have asked to pray for you and tell them how you are progressing. If you need any kind of encouragement, share that need with your prayer partner.

THE BIBLE TEACHING

This section comments on the Scripture and draws meaning from it.

—Write notes in the margin as you read. What questions arise? What additional research and study would be useful? What new insights are you gaining?

—The Bible is not written simply for knowledge. It is intended to inspire you to action. How might you put your new insights to work for you in your life? Begin to plan what you might do this very day to be a disciple of Jesus Christ in the world.

MARKS OF DISCIPLESHIP

The "Marks of Discipleship" summarize major characteristics of the disciple of Jesus Christ and emphasize the practice of discipleship.

—Seek a connection between "Marks of Discipleship" and "Our Human Condition."

—In instances that call for practicing discipleship in a specific way, be creative in thinking about how you can accomplish the goals.

—Move from your comfortable place of study out into the world to practice discipleship.

IF YOU WANT TO KNOW MORE

This section provides practice in using reference materials and in procuring information.

—Take careful notes of your research and study.

—Review your notes that contain questions from your daily reading and make that a focus of your research.

—Scan the information in this section. Some of it is useful at more than one point in the study.

AS YOU STUDY

MARKING YOUR BIBLE

Start DISCIPLE study with a fresh, unmarked Bible so that you approach the Scripture anew, without the influence of earlier notations and markings. Mark your Bible to turn it into a personalized study Bible.

- —Use colored pencils or highlighters, different colors to indicate different kinds of information or reasons for marking.

- —Know why you are marking particular material:
  - What you mark may differ from one type of biblical literature to another.
  - You may choose to mark words or phrases that give clues to the writer's message, names of people and places, sequence in the action, verses that have special meaning for you.

- —Resist the temptation to mark the familiar simply because it is familiar.

- —Indicate new insights or points about which you have questions.

- —Identify passages to memorize.

Ask friends whether they have any advice regarding how they mark their Bibles when reading and studying.

APPROACHING SCRIPTURE

- —Do not rely on your familiarity with Scripture or on study done previously. Come to each lesson and its daily assignments as a beginner, as though you were reading the Scripture passages for the first time even if it is not the first time.

- —Work to identify and organize the information gathered as you study. Use a notebook to do the following:

- Make time charts.
- Develop glossaries of words.
- List key persons and events.
- Identify and discuss biblical and theological ideas.
- Establish the setting of the Scriptures being studied.
- Make connections to other Scriptures and to life situations.
- Discuss insights, experiences, feelings.

—Interpret the text in terms of the meaning originally intended. Try to imagine Bible characters without the knowledge that you possess "after the fact," and attempt to separate your twenty-first-century Christian faith from the Old Testament faith in God. Use suggested reference materials to help you reconstruct in your mind the geographical, cultural, and historical milieu of the time of the Scripture.

PREPARING QUESTIONS AND PONDERING THE LESSON

As you read the Scriptures, questions will naturally pop into your mind. Sometimes they will be fleeting and quickly lost. Learning to capture your questions and properly form them can be one of the most useful skills for studying Scripture.

—Be clear about what you want to accomplish through the questions you prepare.

—Keep in mind the following:
- Questions can help you think.
- Questions can open your mind to new insights or knowledge.
- Questions can enable the examining of an idea, an understanding, an assumption.
- Questions often require probing more deeply into a subject.

Various kinds of questions serve various purposes. Write questions with specific functions in mind. Consider the following:

—If your purpose is to gather or call to mind certain information, write questions that use recall, ask for facts, or require a specific correct answer.

—If your purpose is to organize data, write questions that call for describing, comparing, or contrasting data.

—If your purpose is to analyze a situation or an action, write questions that call for explaining or giving reasons related to the situation or action.

—If your purpose is to make connections or draw conclusions, write questions that call for summarizing or stating the relationship or connection among previously unrelated data.

—If your purpose is to evaluate or make judgments, write questions that ask which choice is best with regard to specific criteria.

—If your purpose is to speculate about an outcome or a situation, write open-ended questions that allow for imagination and the identification of many possibilities.

When writing questions, keep these considerations in mind:

—Generally, yes-or-no questions are too specific and tend to close off an issue from further probing.

—A question is generally poor when no answer is possible or when the answer is too self-evident, too involved, or too vague.

—A good mixture of questions deals with information as well as with feelings and experiences.

—The best questions are stated simply and have only one focus.

—A good question often refers to earlier study and stimulates further inquiry.

—Key words for factual questions are *what, where, when, why, who,* and *how.*

INTERACTING WITH OTHERS

Although you have found it necessary to complete DISCIPLE Bible Study alone, remember that this study is about living in community. Who are the people in your daily life? Who are the spiritual friends who give your life meaning? To whom do you turn to meet your emotional needs? Who are the acquaintances who can benefit from time spent with you? Fellowship, trust, and caring will deepen as you share what you have learned about God's Word and about yourself.

—Search for ways to talk with others about your Bible study. Perhaps there are occasions when family members and friends can be invited for a time of relaxed visiting, playing, and eating together.

—You may choose to celebrate holidays or events that are special to family and friends. The point of such gatherings is to have leisure time together for getting to know one another better, so it's probably best to keep the occasions informal and fairly simple.

RESOURCES FOR FURTHER KNOWLEDGE

Many resources for specific research purposes are suggested throughout the Study Manual, but the following additional resources may also be helpful in generally increasing Bible knowledge:

—*Eerdmans Dictionary of the Bible,* edited by David Noel Freedman (William B. Eerdman, 2000).

—*The Women's Bible Commentary,* edited by Carol A. Newsom and Sharon H. Ringe (Westminster/ John Knox Press, 1992).

—*The Macmillan Bible Atlas* (Third Edition), by Yohanan Aharoni and Michael Avi-Yonah; revised by Anson F. Rainey and Ze'ev Safrai (Macmillan Publishing Company, 1993).

—*Reading Scripture as the Word of God* (Second Edition), by George Martin (Servant Books, 1975, 1982).

WEEK'S ENDING

OPENING PRAYER

Situate yourself comfortably in a location that allows you to close out all those things that distract you from contemplating God's Word. Quiet yourself. Begin to think about God and all of the blessings that come from God. Meditate on the word of the week. When you are ready, begin simply to talk to God about your Bible study and how it related to the activities of your week. Ask God to help you pull together all that you have read in the Bible and in the Study Manual and begin to formulate a plan for your life this coming week.

SCRIPTURE AND STUDY MANUAL

During this time, review the reading in your Study Manual, recall what you have done during the week, and skim your notes and questions. If you would like, you may also choose to view the video or listen to the audio. Afterward, identify, clarify, organize, and master information that you have gathered in your study. Move beyond information to meaning. Guard against simply repeating what you have already done during the week; instead, use it to imagine how God wants you to live from now on, when alone and with your faith community.

ENCOUNTER THE WORD

In this exercise, you will focus on a selected passage from the assigned Scripture. Note that you are instructed to read aloud. The Word of God has been read aloud from the very beginning. This practice helps God's people feel that the Scripture is meant for them. Note that our ears often attend to something that our eyes do not notice. Meaning is gained or expanded. Poetry is experienced more fully, and narrative becomes story. Exhortation attains authority. If you enjoy the practice of reading Scripture aloud, you might choose to purchase or borrow a recorded version of the Bible.

MARKS OF DISCIPLESHIP

Consider what it means to be a disciple. Review the work you have done in this section of the Study Manual. It is important to make a connection between the "Marks of Discipleship" and "Our Human Condition," stated at the beginning of each lesson. This review process will help you relate your Bible study to your relationships with others in your life. Keep in mind that the point of this section and of DISCIPLE Bible Study, in general, is to become a disciple of Jesus Christ.

CONTEMPLATION AT WEEK'S END

At this time, consider what you knew about the week's Bible passages before you studied them. Compare this with what you now know after you have studied them. How did the study affect your spiritual life? Meditate on your growth.

PRAYER CHECK

At the beginning of each week, you are asked to write some prayer concerns in your Study Manual. It is good at the end of the week to review these and check to see whether any answers have been presented or are emerging.

CLOSING PRAYER

Close the session with a prayer. Consider writing all of your closing and opening prayers in a notebook. If you do this, you will have at the end of your study a journal of your prayer life and a prayer guide that you can use many times afterward. If you enjoy music, you might consider singing a favorite hymn.

DISCIPLE

THE OLD TESTAMENT

Summary Sessions

1 INTRODUCTION: THE BIBLICAL WORD

ENCOUNTER THE WORD

Scripture Selection: Psalm 84

Read the passage silently. Then read it aloud and be alert to sounds, smells, sights, tastes, and touches. List what you heard or experienced through the senses.

SUMMARY POINTS

— The reading of Scripture calls us to wrestle with the text in light of the community around us.

— Reading the Scriptures in community lets us know that we are not alone.

— We follow a host of ancestors who attempted to discern God's activity in the past.

— We belong to one another in a global mission seeking to participate in God's mission around the world.

— We read the Bible as a means of being faithful.

— We read the Bible to hear the stories that help us find our own voices and direction.

— The living Word of God helps us discern the spirit of God's Word for our world.

CONTEMPLATION AT WEEK'S END

• **Why do you read the Bible?**

- **How can you study the Bible alone while remembering that you are not isolated in the faith?**

- **How can you turn your new biblical knowledge to the benefit of God's creation?**

PRAYER CHECK

Turn to "Prayer concerns for this week" in your Study Manual. Review all of your petitions for yourself, intercession for others, joys, and praises. Have there been any reports of God's response? Do you need to remain steadfast and patient with these particular prayers?

CLOSING PRAYER

Giver of the Word, thank you for helping me study your Word this week. Forgive me for being unable to pay attention as thoroughly as I wished to be, and help me be more diligent as I move forward. I recognize that even as I study alone, I am a member of my faith community. Teach me more about growing in faith with the people I love. And through time, let me discover, accept, and appreciate the authority of your Word for my life. Help me discern ways that I can turn what I learn into actions that build your kingdom. Amen.

2 THE CREATING GOD

ENCOUNTER THE WORD

Scripture Selection: Psalm 8 or Psalm 100

Read the passages aloud, then memorize either psalm.

SUMMARY POINTS

—The Creation stories of Genesis are among many ancient Creation stories.

—These stories have many similarities: sequence of days; darkness; division of the waters; and light existing before the creation of the sun, moon, and stars.

—But in the Genesis stories, God acts alone; and Creation is God's doing, not a result of conflict among many gods.

—The Creation stories of Genesis were radical, and they challenged the ancient world.

—Genesis 1 and 2 point out that God is unlike all of the other gods and that humanity, being made in God's image, is in relationship with God. This relationship between God and humanity will form the backdrop for the rest of the Bible.

CONTEMPLATION AT WEEK'S END

• **What differences do you see between the two Creation accounts in Genesis 1 and Genesis 2?**

DISCIPLE: Becoming Disciples Through Bible Study

• What does understanding Genesis 1–2 as a backdrop for the rest of the Bible say about God and our relationship with God?

• How does Genesis challenge the Babylonian Creation story in its portrayal of God and God's relationship to humans?

PRAYER CHECK

Turn to "Prayer concerns for this week" in your Study Manual. Review all of your petitions for yourself, intercession for others, joys, and praises. Have there been any reports of God's response? Do you need to remain steadfast and patient with these particular prayers?

CLOSING PRAYER

Creator God, studying the beginnings of your universe makes me think of my own beginnings. I marvel at the magnificence of your creation. That you have made me to be with you and your people is a wonder to me. Your loving work in creation makes me want to join with others in stewardship of the earth. I want to sing praises to you and make others to marvel and worship you, too. Amen.

3 THE REBEL PEOPLE

ENCOUNTER THE WORD

Scripture Selection: Genesis 9:1-19

Read the passage aloud. Contemplate these questions: What does this passage tell me about God? What does this passage tell me about Noah? How am I like Noah? What does this passage tell me about the relationship between God and me?

SUMMARY POINTS

— The theological messages of Genesis 3–11 form the basis of the Bible's overall message.

— The central question these chapters wrestle with is: What does God want us to know about God and God's world?

— These early chapters of Genesis connect the story of Creation to the story of Israel's ancestors.

— The stories describe the fall of humanity and the spread of sin in the world.

— These stories of humanity's rebellion and God's response set the stage for the story of God's attempts to reconcile the world

CONTEMPLATION AT WEEK'S END

• **Ask yourself: Why do I continue in sin, when I want to do only God's will?**

• Ask yourself: How can I become reconciled to God?

PRAYER CHECK

Turn to "Prayer concerns for this week" in your Study Manual. Review all of your petitions for yourself, intercession for others, joys, and praises. Have there been any reports of God's response? Do you need to remain steadfast and patient with these particular prayers?

CLOSING PRAYER

Oh, Lord, I often think too highly of my own mind; and I imagine that I can control my will for only good purposes. In that, I am frequently wrong. Help me accept that I can often stray from your path into sin when I do not let you be my guide. Please guide me this day and all of the days that follow in this week. Amen.

4 THE CALLED PEOPLE

ENCOUNTER THE WORD

Scripture Selection: Genesis 32:9-32

Read the passage aloud. What does this passage say about God? What does this passage say about human beings? What does this passage say about the relationship between God and human beings?

SUMMARY POINTS

— Sarah and Rebekah are often overlooked as partners in fulfilling the covenant promises.

— In the story of Sarai and Abram, God makes it clear that they are covenantal partners.

— God blesses Abraham and Sarah with a son, Isaac, who is a sign that God's promise will be fulfilled.

— The story of Rebekah and Isaac is another case of childlessness followed by a miraculous conception.

— While pregnant with twins, Rebekah is visited by God and told of God's plan. She takes the initiative and works to preserve Jacob as the promise, and the future, of Israel.

CONTEMPLATION AT WEEK'S END

• **How do you see God partnering with the characters in these stories to bring about God's promise?**

• **What role does each of the characters play?**

• **God recruited many partners. Who is available in your life to work with you in partnership with God. What can you do together?**

PRAYER CHECK

Turn to "Prayer concerns for this week" in your Study Manual. Review all of your petitions for yourself, intercession for others, joys, and praises. Have there been any reports of God's response? Do you need to remain steadfast and patient with these particular prayers?

CLOSING PRAYER

O God, I look all about and see how wonderfully you created this beautiful world and then created humankind to covenant with you in nurturing and sustaining it. I want to answer your call, but I need for you to instruct me in how I can best be your partner. Let me help. Show me the way. Amen.

5 GOD HEARS THE CRY

ENCOUNTER THE WORD

Scripture Selection: Exodus 3:1–4:17

Read the passage silently, writing down new insights and questions. Rewrite this passage, envisioning what seems to be the central idea and what meaning the passage might have for the church today. Ask yourself: What is the meaning of the passage for me?

SUMMARY POINTS

— In the Book of Exodus, those living as slaves in Egypt have no memory of God or of God's salvation history.

— God enters human history to save the Israelite people from slavery and death and to create a new future by fulfilling past promises to their ancestors.

— Through Moses, God leads the Israelites out of the land of Egypt and through the Red Sea.

— Why is the night of Passover different from all other nights? The Passover creates hope, since the recounting of past salvation also leads to a future vision, when all evil will be destroyed as Pharaoh and his army were.

CONTEMPLATION AT WEEK'S END

• **How is Exodus a story of divine memory and action?**

• Why is the night of Passover different from all other nights?

• Why does Passover have significance for Christians as well as for Jews?

PRAYER CHECK

Turn to "Prayer concerns for this week" in your Study Manual. Review all of your petitions for yourself, intercession for others, joys, and praises. Have there been any reports of God's response? Do you need to remain steadfast and patient with these particular prayers?

CLOSING PRAYER

Many times, I have felt humiliated, exploited, and truly frightened. I have wanted to run away. But to where? And how to do it? You, my God, have come to deliver me. I appear before you now because you have saved me time after time. Thank you, Divine Protector, for the assurance that you will never abandon me. Amen.

6 GOD SENDS THE LAW

ENCOUNTER THE WORD

Scripture Selection: Deuteronomy 8

Read the passage aloud. Read it aloud a second time from a different Bible version, and ask yourself these questions: What does this passage tell me about God? What does this passage tell me about people? What does this passage say about the relationship between God and people?

SUMMARY POINTS

—God sends the Law for the journey from slavery in Egypt to freedom in the Promised Land. The Law is set within the context of the Torah. The narratives tell us why we should follow the laws.

—The Decalogue, or Ten Commandments, offers general principles concerning what is required to live in relationship with God. It is possible to know the letter of the Law but fail to understand the spirit of the Law.

—The rationale for the Law brings responsibilities under God's covenant and the requirement to act in certain ways before God, with families and neighbors alike.

—To be a person of faith is not just a matter of what we believe; it is also a matter of how we behave.

CONTEMPLATION AT WEEK'S END

• **How can understanding the spirit of the Law affect the way we interpret and live out the Law, especially the Ten Commandments?**

• Firmly knowing that we do not live in isolation from other men and women, consider that the Law is not just about how we relate to God; it is about how we live and work with everyone else in our world. How can you use the Law to be a witness of God's love and a good disciple of Jesus Christ?

PRAYER CHECK

Turn to "Prayer concerns for this week" in your Study Manual. Review all of your petitions for yourself, intercession for others, joys, and praises. Have there been any reports of God's response? Do you need to remain steadfast and patient with these particular prayers?

CLOSING PRAYER

O Great Law Giver, when left on my own, I fall into chaos and self-destruction. I flail about without direction. My personal trauma brings trouble and grief to those around me. No one is served by my disobedience. Please give me the wisdom and the will to follow your commands and to have order in my life. Amen.

7 WHEN GOD DRAWS NEAR

ENCOUNTER THE WORD

Scripture Selection: Exodus 40:16-38

Read the passage silently. Then read the passage aloud, being alert to sounds, smells, sights, tastes, and touches. Note instances involving the senses and answer this question: What can I learn about God from this Scripture?

SUMMARY POINTS

— The covenantal relationship with God and God's people called for special responsibilities: to build a structure that would allow God to dwell among them, and to observe a liturgy that would help the people live up to their responsibilities.

— The sacrificial system provided a type of communication between the people and God. Through the act of atonement and the process of achieving and maintaining oneness and reconciliation with God, a right relationship with God was achieved.

— The covenantal relationship with God reminds us of our ongoing responsibility to God.

— These priestly laws also remind us of the importance of worship and that the way we live our lives should itself be an act of worship.

CONTEMPLATION AT WEEK'S END

• **What did receiving the Law and the liturgy at the same time accomplish for the Israelites?**

• What is the connection between atonement and the Law? between atonement and the liturgy?

• Imagine some ways that you can be at one, not only with God but also with your family and friends. Is there one person with whom you need to have better communication and understanding? What do you need to do to achieve reconciliation?

PRAYER CHECK

Turn to "Prayer concerns for this week" in your Study Manual. Review all of your petitions for yourself, intercession for others, joys, and praises. Have there been any reports of God's response? Do you need to remain steadfast and patient with these particular prayers?

CLOSING PRAYER

Redeemer God, I come to you this moment, with my head cast down in shame and sorrow and my arms raised pleading for you to hear my song of penitence and to accept my worship of you. I ask you to receive my sin offering and to make me whole. May we celebrate atonement together. Amen.

8 THE PEOPLE WITHOUT A KING

Scripture Selection: Joshua 24:1-28

Read the passage aloud. Imagine yourself telling this story to a small group of friends. What do you want your listeners to learn about God? What do you want your listeners to understand about themselves? What do you want your listeners to know about the relationship between God and human beings? Now tell the story about God and Joshua and the tribes, aloud, in your own words.

SUMMARY POINTS

—The Promised Land was lost because God's chosen people and their ancestors failed to keep the covenant they had made with God.

—The narrative of Israel's experience in the land of Canaan is called the Deuteronomistic History. This narration reads more like a confession of sin than a celebration of Israel's past.

—Joshua's warnings of keeping the covenant resulted in a renewal of the covenant. However, the period of history from the death of Joshua to the beginning of David's reign was a seemingly endless cycle, moving from sin to punishment and back again.

—Israel's failure to acknowledge the rule of God allowed evil to reign supreme.

CONTEMPLATION AT WEEK'S END

• **"In those days there was no king in Israel; all the people did what was right in their own eyes." How does this statement describe how God's chosen people came to lose their promised land?**

• **What role did Joshua and the judges play in Israel's experience? What role can you play in your community?**

• **Are you, like Joshua, called to be a leader? If not, what is your calling to be a faithful follower?**

PRAYER CHECK

Turn to "Prayer concerns for this week" in your Study Manual. Review all of your petitions for yourself, intercession for others, joys, and praises. Have there been any reports of God's response? Do you need to remain steadfast and patient with these particular prayers?

CLOSING PRAYER

Amazing God, I appear before you, willing to accept any leadership role you offer me. But I will need your constant guidance. Lord, if your will for me is to be a spiritual leader by demonstrating trust and obedience, that will be more than enough for me. Amen.

9 THE PEOPLE WITH A KING

ENCOUNTER THE WORD

Scripture Selection: 1 Kings 9:1-9

Read the passage aloud. Write down 1) the insights you received from the Scripture; 2) the central idea of the passage; 3) the meaning the passage has for today's world; and 4) the personal message of the passage.

SUMMARY POINTS

—While being threatened with invasion from their enemies, God's people saw military victory as their only hope.

—God's people asked Samuel to appoint a king to govern them as other nations were governed.

—Samuel reluctantly anointed a king. In succession, Saul, David, and Solomon served as kings.

—The unification of the tribes was short-lived, and the monarchy was divided between the Northern Kingdom of Israel and the Southern Kingdom of Judah. The classical prophets were active during this period of the Divided Monarchy.

—Political instability eventually led to the fall of both Israel and Judah.

—Exiled in Babylon, each of the kings of Israel and Judah contributed in some way to his nation's slide toward destruction.

CONTEMPLATION AT WEEK'S END

• **Why did the people desire a king? What was their experience of having a king?**

• What impact did writing from the perspective of the Exile have on how the history of the kings and God's people was told?

• Contrast the kingship of the Old Testament with what it means to be royalty today. What comparisons and contrasts can be made with our democratically elected presidents? What do we need and expect from our leaders today?

PRAYER CHECK

Turn to "Prayer concerns for this week" in your Study Manual. Review all of your petitions for yourself, intercession for others, joys, and praises. Have there been any reports of God's response? Do you need to remain steadfast and patient with these particular prayers?

CLOSING PRAYER

Dear God, is it any easier to be a national leader today than during your time of the judges and kings? I lift up all of the leaders of the world in prayer and ask you to bless them. I ask you to bless the kings, queens, premiers, and presidents so that all of the people of the world will be blessed through them and know complete peace and security at last. Amen.

10 GOD WARNS THE PEOPLE

ENCOUNTER THE WORD

Scripture Selection: 1 Kings 19:1-18

Try mental drama as you read the passage aloud. Clarify the setting, the characters, and what is going on in the story. Then close your eyes. Imagine what Elijah thought, how he felt, and what he thought about God. Give time for thought after each question. What new insights did you gain into Elijah and into the story?

SUMMARY POINTS

—The historian of First and Second Kings never measures a royal reign by how powerful the king may have been in the world, but by how faithful he was to the Lord.

—Given this criterion, none of the kings in the north, and few in the south, get a passing grade. According to the historian, they did what was evil in the sight of the Lord. Ahab, in particular, was denounced for introducing idol worship.

—At this low point in Israel's history, Elijah hoped to turn the heart of the people back to the one and only true God.

—On Mount Carmel, Elijah asked the people to make a choice about who they would worship: God or Baal. When Baal is silent and God answers with a consuming fire, Elijah's message is heard.

CONTEMPLATION AT WEEK'S END

• **Every era in history has its dangers, and no one today is free of peril. What do we need to be warned about?**

- **What must be happening in the world in order for a prophetic voice to be raised?**

- **What must happen for people to respond to that prophetic voice?**

PRAYER CHECK

Turn to "Prayer concerns for this week" in your Study Manual. Review all of your petitions for yourself, intercession for others, joys, and praises. Have there been any reports of God's response? Do you need to remain steadfast and patient with these particular prayers?

CLOSING PRAYER

God of All, do not let me miss the warnings about my own choices and behavior. Prepare me to hear those who would lead me to the right path for my life. Open my ears to those who would keep me from straying. Let me accept the word of life that leads directly to you. Amen.

11 GOD PUNISHES THE PEOPLE

ENCOUNTER THE WORD

Scripture Selection: Jeremiah 24

Have on hand a scrap of paper and a pencil as you read the passage. Make two columns, one for positive statements and the other for negative ones. For every positive or negative statement, make a mark in the appropriate column. Ask yourself these questions: How do the columns tally? What does this text have to say to the church in our day? If I were to take this passage seriously, what changes would I have to make in my life?

SUMMARY POINTS

—Judah experienced religious reform during the reign of Josiah:
  • Restoration and rededication of the Temple
  • Discovery of the book of the Law, leading to a renewal and reinstitution of religious rites
  • Purging of alien cultic objects from the Temple and demolition of local sanctuaries and high places
  • Institution of a national celebration of Passover

—After the death of Josiah, the nation went downhill quickly; and Jeremiah warned of God's judgment.

—Jerusalem was destroyed and the people were taken into exile. Yet even in the face of the catastrophe and despair, Jeremiah preached and practiced hope.

CONTEMPLATION AT WEEK'S END

• **"Both blessings and disasters are in the hands of the Lord." How do you respond to that statement?**

• According to Second Kings, which gets the people's attention: blessings or disasters? Why?

• What is Jeremiah's response? What conclusions might you make about cause and effect?

PRAYER CHECK

Turn to "Prayer concerns for this week" in your Study Manual. Review all of your petitions for yourself, intercession for others, joys, and praises. Have there been any reports of God's response? Do you need to remain steadfast and patient with these particular prayers?

CLOSING PRAYER

Dear God, please do not let me overlook my failures and wrongdoing. Do not allow me to deny my fault; blame others; or settle into anger, depression, and despair. Before I act, let me consider the consequences and be humbled, chastened, and corrected. Amen.

12 GOD RESTORES THE PEOPLE

ENCOUNTER THE WORD

Scripture Selection: Isaiah 45:1-13

Read the passage aloud. Who is a revered voice of authority in your life? Imagine that person reading this passage. Read the verse again, hearing his or her voice reading, instead of your own. Then answer these questions: What does this passage tell us about God? What does this passage tell us about human beings (as represented by Cyrus)? What does this passage tell us about the relationship between God and Cyrus (as a representative human being)?

SUMMARY POINTS

— God held the people of Judah accountable for their sins. God used the Babylonians to punish the people of Judah.

— The writer of Second Isaiah (Isaiah 40–55) brings a word of hope. The God who acted to destroy Judah was about to restore it.

— The restoration would be at the hands of Cyrus, king of the Persians, and through the life of an unknown figure called the "suffering servant," who suffers innocently and whose suffering benefits others.

— Suffering is not necessarily the sign of God's disfavor and punishment; rather, God may well redeem suffering for the sake of the world. God can work a redemptive purpose in even the most broken of persons and situations.

— Jeremiah 31 affirms that, after the exile, God will establish a new covenant with the people, a covenant written on people's hearts.

CONTEMPLATION AT WEEK'S END

• **The same God who holds people accountable for their behaviors is also gracious and forgiving. How was this played out in the life of the people of Judah? How is this still played out in the life of God's people?**

• When in your personal sin have you been humbled, pardoned, or comforted?

• Do you have an opportunity to be a conduit of God's forgiveness and comfort to another? With whom can you share this encouraging word of prophesy from Isaiah?

PRAYER CHECK

Turn to "Prayer concerns for this week" in your Study Manual. Review all of your petitions for yourself, intercession for others, joys, and praises. Have there been any reports of God's response? Do you need to remain steadfast and patient with these particular prayers?

CLOSING PRAYER

Father, our darkest moments of wrongdoing and despair are often immediately followed by our brightest moments of realization that you are present with us, loving us, forgiving us, comforting us. Thank you for turning our sadness into dance and our sorrow into joy. I sing praises to you. I give you thanks forever. Amen.

13 SONGS OF THE HEART

ENCOUNTER THE WORD

Scripture Selection: Psalm 22

Read the psalm aloud. Use these questions to work through the psalm in blocks of verses: What does the psalm tell us about God? What does the psalm tell us about us? What does the psalm tell us about the relationship between God and us? Pick one or two verses that are most appealing to you or that you think might be most life-changing for you, then memorize them.

SUMMARY POINTS

—The psalms mirror our hearts and speak our deepest thoughts. They can teach our hearts about whom God is and what God has done. They also teach us how to pray.

—Psalms of praise (Psalm 147 and 116)
 • Often used in corporate worship
 • Two types of psalms of praise: descriptive—praise the attributes of God; declarative—give thanks for a specific act
 • Teach us whom God is

—Psalms of lament (Psalm 13 and 74)
 • Two types: solitary voice—"rescue me"; corporate voice—the people ask God to intervene
 • Prayers asking God for help

CONTEMPLATION AT WEEK'S END

• **Why do we so often turn to the psalms?**

• **How have the psalms taught you to pray?**

• **Psalms are often shared among the faithful in order to encourage and to strengthen. Review what you wrote in the Study Manual on pages 95–97. Remember someone now who can use a word of encouragement and strengthening. Send that person a verse from Psalms that means a lot to you. Alternatively, write a verse of your own and send it to that person.**

PRAYER CHECK

Turn to "Prayer concerns for this week" in your Study Manual. Review all of your petitions for yourself, intercession for others, joys, and praises. Have there been any reports of God's response? Do you need to remain steadfast and patient with these particular prayers?

CLOSING PRAYER

Dear Savior, in my many moods and for my many situations, I need a different word from you. Give me a lament for my sorrow, a word of repentance for my guilt, praise for my joy, wisdom greater than my foolishness, and thanksgiving for all of your blessings bestowed on me. Let me worship you with my whole heart. Amen.

14 THE RIGHTEOUS ARE LIKE A TREE

ENCOUNTER THE WORD

Scripture Selection: Psalm 112

Read the psalm, and identify major ideas. Then put the passage into your own words. Do some verses seem strange to you and difficult to paraphrase? Do some verses seem written especially for you? Select one verse that seems to be advising or guiding you, print it in large letters, and tape it to your bathroom or bedroom mirror for contemplation every day this week.

SUMMARY POINTS

—The victory of Cyrus brought not only a new political order to the ancient Near East, but it also brought new theological choices for God's people.

—Major concerns:
  • Temple worship. Some return to build; some stay behind to help fund the project.
  • Defining community boundaries in the midst of various groups: returning exiles, exiles living outside the land (Diaspora), adversaries, and foreigners.
  • How to live faithfully and practice righteousness.

—Deeply influenced by international traditions, the Book of Proverbs suggests that right living comes not by excluding the foreigner but by adapting some of the insights of other traditions and marshalling them under "the fear of the Lord."

CONTEMPLATION AT WEEK'S END

• **What were the major concerns of the postexilic community, and how did the people deal with them?**

- **Remember that discipleship involves living in community. What are some ways in which you can be righteous, frugal, generous, and considerate of others' needs?**

PRAYER CHECK

Turn to "Prayer concerns for this week" in your Study Manual. Review all of your petitions for yourself, intercession for others, joys, and praises. Have there been any reports of God's response? Do you need to remain steadfast and patient with these particular prayers?

CLOSING PRAYER

God, life provides me with hourly opportunities to be unchaste, idle, false, foolish, disobedient. Thank you for giving me clear ordinances and commands for right living. Help me reject behaviors that at first seem to offer some joy or advantage but that ultimately mess up my life and destroy my good relationship with you. Let me partner with you for my own well-being. Amen.

15 WHEN TROUBLE COMES

ENCOUNTER THE WORD

Scripture Selection: Job 3–42 (see the dramatic reading in the Study Manual)

Put these three steps on a sheet of paper, then read the passage.

1. Identify the different kinds of counsel offered by Job's friends.
2. Observe how their explanations are still used today.
3. Consider the sense in which the explanations are partly true but not completely appropriate.

SUMMARY POINTS

—A study of the Book of Job presents a number of challenges:
  • Reconciling the compliant Job of the prologue with the complaining Job of the epilogue
  • Understanding the complex depiction of God
  • Making sense of the sophisticated and often ambiguous poetic language

—The book begins and ends with a prose narrative. A long poem stands in between, written as a conversation among Job and three friends. A monologue by Elihu follows. God then speaks to Job out of the whirlwind, and the poetry ends with a last word from Job.

—The opening question, "Does Job fear God for nothing?" is not the only question on the table. Job wants to know why God should be feared at all if God is indeed so oblivious to injustice and suffering.

—Job's friends insist that he must have sinned and is getting what he deserves.

—Job demands an answer from God. God answers with a litany of questions and imperatives. In response, Job sees himself and God in a new way.

CONTEMPLATION AT WEEK'S END

• **What do the responses of Job, Job's friends, and God convey about the message of the book? How do you respond to Job's suffering?**

• **You have probably heard about the human pain threshold and know something about your own. Consider a parallel concept for suffering, and evaluate your own ability to handle suffering.**

• **Do you know some people who seem to break down quickly in the face of adversity and other people who never complain or whine? What role can God, prayer, and faith friends serve in times of suffering?**

PRAYER CHECK

Turn to "Prayer concerns for this week" in your Study Manual. Review all of your petitions for yourself, intercession for others, joys, and praises. Have there been any reports of God's response? Do you need to remain steadfast and patient with these particular prayers?

CLOSING PRAYER

Merciful God, help me resist the temptation to recite a litany about fairness when adversity and suffering come my way. May I remember that trouble comes to all those who draw breath. May I choose to respond with creativity rather than bitterness, praise songs rather than whining, and laughter rather than weeping. Let me remember that, with sorrow, comes comfort. Amen.

16 PEOPLE HOPE FOR A SAVIOR

ENCOUNTER THE WORD

Scripture Selection: Isaiah 65:17-25

Read the passage aloud, being alert to sounds, sights, smells, touches, and tastes as you read. To which senses does the Scripture appeal, and what feelings do you experience as you read it?

SUMMARY POINTS

Daniel is composed of two kinds of literature:

—The hero stories (1-6)
   • Arose in circumstances characterized by Diaspora existence, cross-cultural contact, and uneven distribution of power
   • Contain a call to resist and defy foreign power (i.e., refusing the king's food and wine)
   • Message: Remain faithful in times of trial

—The visions (7-12)
   • Describe conflict
   • Involve both earthly and heavenly figures
   • Give reassurance that God is in charge
   • Message: Be boldly defiant because God has ultimate dominion over all
   • The Book of Daniel calls us to speak truth to power.

CONTEMPLATION AT WEEK'S END

• **Discuss the overall theme of Daniel. Themes are sometimes obscured in dreams and prophesies, ancient images, and concealed symbols. After picking through them all this week, what has been revealed to you?**

• How does your life sometimes appear confused with symbols, dreams, and visions? How do you make your way through all of them to find a path forward? How can you help others find their way?

• How can you be an interpreter of dreams and hidden messages?

PRAYER CHECK

Turn to "Prayer concerns for this week" in your Study Manual. Review all of your petitions for yourself, intercession for others, joys, and praises. Have there been any reports of God's response? Do you need to remain steadfast and patient with these particular prayers?

CLOSING PRAYER

Ancient of Days, I am so tied up in the doings and activities of the present moment that I can scarcely even think about the future—let alone envision it and understand it. The trials of my day seem too dense to see through to a brighter future. But the story of Daniel gives me courage to live well—if not easily. And Daniel gives me hope. Thank you for a brighter tomorrow. Amen.

17 THE TIME OF TRANSITION

Scripture Selection: Jonah 3:10–4:11

Read the passage silently, and answer these questions: What happened in this story? What did the story likely say to its first hearers? What did the writer of the story want to say for God? What is the story's central purpose? What does the story mean for you and your life? Call a trusted friend and discuss questions and thoughts about the meaning of these verses for your life.

SUMMARY POINTS

—The Persian period was a time of transition for the Jews. During that time, more Jews lived outside the historical land of Israel than inside it. These circumstances created challenges for the Jews. The stories of Esther and Jonah sought to address the questions Jews were facing.

—The purpose of the story of Esther was to teach a lesson: how Jews were to function successfully in a Gentile world. Without mentioning God or religion, the writer promotes the idea that Jews and Gentiles can live together harmoniously and with mutual respect in the Diaspora world.

—The story of Jonah is a deceptively simple tale about a prophet named Jonah. Through use of broad humor, the author makes a serious point and addresses the question: Is God the God only of the Israelites, or does God's power extend to other people? The answer is that God is the God of both Jews and Gentiles, and God's power and mercy extend over the whole world.

- **During the Persian period, the Jews experienced a time of transition and multiple challenges. How did the messages of Esther and Jonah address these challenges?**

- **The apostle Paul was not the first to go to the Gentiles with the message of salvation. Compare your New Testament knowledge with these Old Testament stories that don't even mention a future Messiah.**

- **Explore what it means to be a disciple of Jesus Christ in a modern world of diverse faiths.**

PRAYER CHECK

Turn to "Prayer concerns for this week" in your Study Manual. Review all of your petitions for yourself, intercession for others, joys, and praises. Have there been any reports of God's response? Do you need to remain steadfast and patient with these particular prayers?

CLOSING PRAYER

Like Esther and Jonah, I am increasingly encountering people in my community who do not know you. Their faith and customs are strange to me. Father, every day help me know how I am to be a disciple of your Son in a multicultural neighborhood. As Jesus reflected your glory and bore the stamp of your nature, let me graciously reflect your glory and bear the stamp of your love in my neighborhood. Amen.

DISCIPLE

THE NEW TESTAMENT

Summary Sessions

18 RADICAL DISCIPLESHIP

ENCOUNTER THE WORD

Scripture Selection: Matthew 20:1-16

Read the passage aloud. Imagine yourself being in the crowd listening to Jesus. Imagine that, after he has told this parable, you and a friend discuss these questions: What does this parable tell us about God? What does this parable tell us about human beings? What does this parable tell us about the relationship between God and human beings?

SUMMARY POINTS

—Five major themes emerge in Matthew's portrait of Jesus:
1. Jesus is a teacher, which is shown in the emphasis on teaching throughout the Gospel and in the Great Commission.
2. Less emphasis is placed on miracles because miracle stories introduce questions about discipleship.
3. Jesus is the Jewish messiah, sent by a Jewish God, in fulfillment of the Jewish Scriptures.
4. Emphasis is placed on a different kind of righteousness. A disciple's righteousness must be better, greater, and more effective than the Law requires.
5. The Gospel's universal mission is found and cultivated in particular contexts.

—Matthew's teaching calls for radical discipleship.

CONTEMPLATION AT WEEK'S END

• **What does the term *radical discipleship* mean to you?**

- **What will you do to be a radical disciple? How will you live in your work community, your family, your faith community?**

- **Choose one or two of the communities in which you live, and ask members this question: Is there something more I can do to make our community better? How can you respond to their suggestions?**

PRAYER CHECK
_____

Turn to "Prayer concerns for this week" in your Study Manual. Review all of your petitions for yourself, intercession for others, joys, and praises. Have there been any reports of God's response? Do you need to remain steadfast and patient with these particular prayers?

CLOSING PRAYER
_____

Dear Creator of the Kingdom, I have heard clearly this week that to be a disciple is not just to *be* but to *do*. I will do, with your guidance and help. Lord, make me more aware than I have ever been of the needs of my community. Make me more knowledgeable of the example Jesus Christ has set. And make me more responsive in every way. Amen.

19 MOUNTING CONTROVERSY

ENCOUNTER THE WORD

Scripture Selection: Matthew 26:69-75

Silently read the passage, then read it aloud. If possible, record your reading and listen to the recording. In your reading, listen for descriptions of sounds, sights, and touches; and list the various senses identified. Imagine being in the courtyard that night. What would you be thinking and feeling? Then silently read Mark 14:66-72; Luke 22:54-62; and John 18:15-18, 25-27. How much richer is the story when told in four different voices?

SUMMARY POINTS

— In Matthew, the rejection of Jesus begins almost immediately. While the magi bring precious gifts to the child, Herod seeks to take his life. Jesus' birth evokes both acceptance and rejection the same as his death and resurrection and his deeds.

— According to Matthew, the Pharisees are more concerned with proper observance of the Law than with helping others. Because of this, the Jewish leaders are portrayed as hypocrites. Opposition to Jesus and his criticism of the Jewish leaders builds.

— Jesus cleanses the Temple.

— Jesus tells parables that portray his opponents in a negative way.

— "Seven Woes" are pronounced against the Pharisees.

— The problem for Jesus in Matthew is never the Jews or the Jewish religion. The problem is the Jewish leadership. Matthew affirms Judaism, but as it is interpreted by Jesus.

CONTEMPLATION AT WEEK'S END

• **Consider the tension between Jesus and the Jewish leadership. What does Jesus' criticism of the Jewish leadership say to those who would be his disciples?**

• **How do you experience your discipleship as threatening?**

• **In what ways does your discipleship require sacrifice? If you can think of no sacrificial elements, consider what that says about your level of commitment.**

PRAYER CHECK

Turn to "Prayer concerns for this week" in your Study Manual. Review all of your petitions for yourself, intercession for others, joys, and praises. Have there been any reports of God's response? Do you need to remain steadfast and patient with these particular prayers?

CLOSING PRAYER

God of the Cross, I come humbly before you this day, knowing that there are no lengths to which you will not go for my benefit. I question my own commitment to you and to my Savior, who went to the cross for my sake. Lord, strengthen my determination to be a follower of Christ, no matter the cost. Help me deny myself that I will not deny my Savior. Amen.

20 THE HIDDEN MESSIAH

ENCOUNTER THE WORD

Scripture Selection: Mark 9:2-13

Read the passage aloud, and engage in a mental drama. Use these statements and questions: Imagine yourself as Peter or James or John on the mountain with Jesus. What are you thinking and feeling as you watch what is happening? Imagine yourself as James or John. What do you think of Peter's suggestion? What are you wondering as you come down the mountain, especially when Jesus tells you not to tell anyone about your experience? Read the story again, with drama.

SUMMARY POINTS

— Mark identifies Jesus as the Christ, the Son of God. In Hebrew, *Christ* means "messiah, one who has been anointed." But Jesus was not the kind of messiah people expected.

— Throughout most of Mark's story, Jesus tries to keep his messianic identity secret. He tells those he healed to say nothing. He even tells his disciples to remain quiet. But the more Jesus told them to keep quiet, the more people proclaimed his miraculous deeds.

— It isn't until his trial before the Sanhedrin that Jesus makes his identity known. And when he does, he is condemned to death.

— At the end of Mark, the women who visited the empty tomb are told to go and tell. Yet they say nothing to anyone. Were they afraid? We too are told to go and tell. What is our response?

CONTEMPLATION AT WEEK'S END

• **Why did Jesus want to keep his identity secret? How would you describe the identity of Christ today?**

• Now that the secret of Christ is out and we are called to tell the story, what is our response?

• Now you are deep into the study of what it means to be a disciple, and this lesson has given a core teaching of the faith: There is Good News to be spread far and wide. Who, when, how will you spread the Good News this week?

PRAYER CHECK

Turn to "Prayer concerns for this week" in your Study Manual. Review all of your petitions for yourself, intercession for others, joys, and praises. Have there been any reports of God's response? Do you need to remain steadfast and patient with these particular prayers?

CLOSING PRAYER

Dear God, I know for certain that the time is fulfilled and your kingdom is at hand. I believe in the gospel, and my joy cannot be contained. I must break out of my quiet zone and tell the Good News. All praise and thanks to you for this great thing you have done! Amen.

21 GOD SEEKS THE LEAST, THE LAST, THE LOST

ENCOUNTER THE WORD

Scripture Selection: Luke 16:19-31

Read the passage, and see whether you noticed anything during this reading that you have not noted before. Then read the story again in at least one other Bible version, and answer these questions: What is the central idea of the passage? What meaning does this passage have for Christians today? What does this passage require of me?

SUMMARY POINTS

— For Luke, Jesus was the Savior who had come to bring Good News to the poor, release to the captives, and salvation to the lost. Beginning with the announcement of Jesus' birth, Luke weaves a story of one who came for the least and the lost.

— Luke demands that those who follow Jesus must do so in the dirty, violent world of hunger, disease, prejudice, and oppression. Discipleship is not just a matter of inward purity; it requires compassionate intervention on behalf of the poor, the hungry, the homeless, and the despised.

— What was the sign that confirmed that the Messiah had come? Jesus told John's followers to go back and tell him that "the blind receive their sight, the lame walk, the lepers are cleansed, the deaf hear, the dead are raised, the poor have good news brought to them."

CONTEMPLATION AT WEEK'S END

• **What image of Jesus is portrayed in Luke?**

• What kind of discipleship does Jesus call for in Luke? What about Luke's story of Jesus' ministry makes you uncomfortable? Why?

• What about Luke's story of Jesus' ministry makes you want to get up immediately and meet the needs of the world? What is stopping you?

PRAYER CHECK

Turn to "Prayer concerns for this week" in your Study Manual. Review all of your petitions for yourself, intercession for others, joys, and praises. Have there been any reports of God's response? Do you need to remain steadfast and patient with these particular prayers?

CLOSING PRAYER

God of Compassion, I am so moved that you have not forgotten the poor, the hungry, those with handicaps, the displaced, the oppressed, the least. You sent Jesus to care for them, but so many of us have forgotten them. Remake me as a disciple today. Give me all I need to serve others. Amen.

22 LIFEGIVER

ENCOUNTER THE WORD

Scripture Selection: John 10:7-18

Read the passage, then study it and rewrite it in your own words. Don't summarize; paraphrase each verse. Now read the same verses in another Bible version and see if it leads you to alter your personal version.

SUMMARY POINTS

— Distinctiveness of John's Gospel:
- No genealogy
- No annunciation; no magi; no birth
- Begins before Creation
- Jesus' ministry lasts three years
- No parables; no exorcisms

— The Gospel of John emphasizes Jesus' power, sovereignty, glory, and divinity at every turn. Jesus is not baptized by John the Baptist. Jesus is not tempted in the wilderness. Jesus is not shown as a victim. Jesus is in control of everything.

— The single message of John is that Jesus and God are one with each other and with all believers.

— The Gospel of John could just as easily be called the Gospel of Life.

— Unlike many New Testament writers, John indicates no belief whatsoever in hell. All judgment takes place in this life. John stresses repeatedly that the life Jesus promises is available now.

— According to John, with Jesus, we have all the life we need.

• **What are the distinctive characteristics of the Gospel of John?**

• **How does the Gospel of John describe the life believers can experience in Jesus Christ? What is your concept of "the good life"?**

• **Compare and contrast your concept with John's Gospel.**

PRAYER CHECK

Turn to "Prayer concerns for this week" in your Study Manual. Review all of your petitions for yourself, intercession for others, joys, and praises. Have there been any reports of God's response? Do you need to remain steadfast and patient with these particular prayers?

CLOSING PRAYER

Lord, help me be the disciple who finds light in a darkened world, spiritual food and drink in a hungry and thirsty world, meaning in a confusing and seemingly meaningless world. Let me be a shepherd in a lost and lonely world. Let me help bring life to others. Amen.

23 ADVOCATE

ENCOUNTER THE WORD

Scripture Selection: John 13:1-20

Read the passage aloud. Identify the details and sequence of the story. Read it again for sounds, smells, sights, tastes, and touches. List all of the ways the story involves the senses. Answer this question: What new understandings came from reading the story this way?

SUMMARY POINTS

—In John, Jesus is the only person in the narrative who has a relationship with the Holy Spirit before the Crucifixion. No one else in the story receives the Holy Spirit until after Jesus is glorified through his crucifixion and resurrection.

—Jesus establishes the future life of the believing community as the household of God. Through language of dwelling or abiding, Jesus speaks of relationship. Jesus comes and dwells among us and makes us children of God. God and Jesus dwell in one another; God, Jesus, and the Holy Spirit dwell in the believers.

—Through the power of the Holy Spirit, the community of Jesus' disciples can carry out the only commandment given in the Gospel of John: Love one another.

CONTEMPLATION AT WEEK'S END

• **What is the role of the Holy Spirit in the life of the believing community and of the disciple?**

• **Think back to the day when you decided to begin this study: What were your reasons for deciding to participate? Did you need reassurance that you are not alone in life, that someone cares, and that you could find evidence of this in the Bible?**

PRAYER CHECK

Turn to "Prayer concerns for this week" in your Study Manual. Review all of your petitions for yourself, intercession for others, joys, and praises. Have there been any reports of God's response? Do you need to remain steadfast and patient with these particular prayers?

CLOSING PRAYER

Father, it is immensely comforting for me to know that Jesus prayed to you for his disciples. I am one of those he entrusted to you. I crave reassurance that you are protecting me from the evil one. I rejoice that, although I am completing this Bible study alone, I am bound by Jesus' prayer to all of the other faithful. Amen.

24 THE EXPLOSIVE POWER OF THE SPIRIT

ENCOUNTER THE WORD

Scripture Selection: Acts 4:32–5:11

Read the passage. Then study it, using these questions: What does this passage say about God? What does this passage say about human beings? What does this passage say about the relationship between God and human beings?

SUMMARY POINTS

— The Book of the Acts of the Apostles describes a dynamic, explosive world where the Spirit of the risen Jesus is active.

— The Spirit is active in proclaiming the name of Jesus, the source of its power; active through the prayers of believers, its means of power; and active in bearing witness to Jesus through preaching and healing, the purpose of its power.

— Acts 1:8 sets the theme for the whole Book of Acts. Then Luke spends the rest of his narrative showing how Jesus' followers are empowered by the Holy Spirit as they witness to the Lord Jesus, even in the midst of opposition and conflict.

CONTEMPLATION AT WEEK'S END

• **How did the early church experience the presence and power of the Holy Spirit?**

• How do you experience the presence and power of the Holy Spirit in your life? Does it call you at the present to wait and be contemplative? Or is it explosive and infectious?

PRAYER CHECK

Turn to "Prayer concerns for this week" in your Study Manual. Review all of your petitions for yourself, intercession for others, joys, and praises. Have there been any reports of God's response? Do you need to remain steadfast and patient with these particular prayers?

CLOSING PRAYER

Dear God, I am reminded by this week's lesson that a great cloud of witnesses has come before me. They healed, converted, served, and changed society. They had no power to do any of that, except by the Holy Spirit. I want to follow their lead, and I have the same power to do so. Bless my discipleship, Lord. Amen.

25 THE GOSPEL PENETRATES THE WORLD

Scripture Selection: Ephesians 1:3-2:10

Read the passage as though it is a letter you have just received from the apostle Paul. Write your reply on a piece of paper. What comments would you make to Paul? What questions would continue your correspondence? How would you tell Paul that you appreciate him?

SUMMARY POINTS

— Acts is the story of those who first proclaimed the story of Jesus. In spite of difficulties, the earliest Christians developed particular strategies for accomplishing their mission to spread the gospel, using missionary teams to spread the gospel and accepting hospitality as an entry point for sharing the gospel.

— The missionary teams prepared the way for sharing the gospel, sustained new communities of believers, and followed up with believers previously visited.

— Learning to manage differences in language, ethnicity, even theological belief, the early church in Acts took seriously the task of proclaiming Christ to the ends of the earth.

CONTEMPLATION AT WEEK'S END

• **What are your thoughts about the strategies the early Christians used to spread the gospel?**

• **What do these strategies teach about how to spread the gospel today?**

• **How can you use these strategies? With whom will you partner to spread the Good News?**

PRAYER CHECK

Turn to "Prayer concerns for this week" in your Study Manual. Review all of your petitions for yourself, intercession for others, joys, and praises. Have there been any reports of God's response? Do you need to remain steadfast and patient with these particular prayers?

CLOSING PRAYER

God, help me be as bold as the apostle Paul in declaring the gospel and converting others for my faith community. Help me overcome the fear that I am unprepared for the work or that people will reject me and my message. Give me confidence that those who are unfamiliar to me can become my friends in Christ Jesus. Let me claim the power of the Holy Spirit within me. Amen.

26 PUT RIGHT WITH GOD THROUGH FAITH

ENCOUNTER THE WORD

Scripture Selection: Romans 4:13–5:5

Read the passage in two or, preferably, three Bible versions. Compare and contrast the complex theological concepts presented there, and answer these questions: What does this passage tell us about God? What does this passage tell us about human beings? What does this passage tell us about the relationship between God and human beings?

SUMMARY POINTS

—The key question that drives the whole letter of Romans is this: Can God be trusted?

—Paul addresses the issues of God's universal justice; God's faithfulness to Israel; and how the death and resurrection of Jesus are to be understood as the fulfillment, rather than the undoing, of all that God has promised Israel from the beginning.

—Why did Paul send this letter to Rome?

—Roman Christians needed to hear that the real Lord—the real giver of peace, justice, and salvation—was Jesus, not Caesar.

—Paul was also writing to appeal for support as he continued his missionary journeys.

—Paul's letter to the Romans confirms that the God who has chosen us freely in love can be trusted.

CONTEMPLATION AT WEEK'S END

• **What points does Paul make in arguing that God can be trusted?**

• Why is the question of whether God can be trusted so crucial for Paul? How is that question still crucial for Christians?

• When you are completely honest with yourself, what questions do you have about belief and what are your trust issues?

PRAYER CHECK

Turn to "Prayer concerns for this week" in your Study Manual. Review all of your petitions for yourself, intercession for others, joys, and praises. Have there been any reports of God's response? Do you need to remain steadfast and patient with these particular prayers?

CLOSING PRAYER

God the Father, I do believe in you and your son Jesus, my savior. Because of my belief, I want to live righteously, but daily I fail. Thank you for giving me peace in knowing that I am justified into right relationship with you, the Creator of all the universe. Amen.

27 A CONGREGATION IN FERMENT

ENCOUNTER THE WORD

Scripture Selection: 1 Corinthians 3:1-23

Read the passage, and rewrite the passage in your own words. Now put your written words away for a few minutes while you read the Summary Points and Contemplation at Week's End. Then pick up and read your paraphrase. What do you see in your written words that indicates your own experiences with church conflicts? What have you learned about working cooperatively?

SUMMARY POINTS

— Paul's first letter to the Corinthians is in response to questions from various leaders in the community with regard to divisions in the community, sexual immorality, lawsuits, and the Lord's supper.

— The main point of Paul's first letter to the Corinthians can be summed up when he says, "All of you be in agreement ... be united in the same mind and the same purpose."

— Central to Paul's teachings to this community were the cross and the resurrection of Christ.

— Paul identifies what is crucial to the church then and today: the unity of the Body.

CONTEMPLATION AT WEEK'S END

• **What were the issues facing the Corinthian congregation?**

• **What was Paul's message?**

• **How is the message of Corinthians relevant to the church today?**

PRAYER CHECK

Turn to "Prayer concerns for this week" in your Study Manual. Review all of your petitions for yourself, intercession for others, joys, and praises. Have there been any reports of God's response? Do you need to remain steadfast and patient with these particular prayers?

CLOSING PRAYER

Dear God, I want to believe that in the church we are all unified in every detail of congregational life. I want to believe it, but I am not really that naive. I know that there are conflicts on many issues. Still, we can find common belief in all things essential. In less important matters, we can listen with respect, debate with dignity, and treat all in love. Help me be a respectful, dignified, and loving disciple. Amen.

28 THE SON SHALL SET US FREE

ENCOUNTER THE WORD

Scripture Selection: Galatians 5:1-13 and 6:1-10

Quickly read the passage. You can see that both are powerful preaching. Imagine that you are preparing to deliver one of these passages as a sermon. Plan the way you will vocalize each word. Which sentences will you emphasize? Where will you pause for effect? Making these decisions requires that you study and understand your text. Now stand and deliver your sermon.

SUMMARY POINTS

—Galatians is an impassioned conversation about the religious and social boundaries of the church.

—Paul insisted that faith in Christ did not obligate Gentiles to convert to Judaism. Following the Law did not bring justification or a proper relationship with God. This is possible through faith alone.

—Justification by faith is not simply about individual salvation, regardless of social differences. It also allows the church to express communal unity in the midst of social diversity. Paul pleads for the erasure of dominance, not the removal of difference.

—Christian faith not only engenders communal harmony but also freedom. Believers have been freed from enslaving forces and freed for loving service to the neighbor.

CONTEMPLATION AT WEEK'S END

• **Relate the freedom that the Christian faith engenders to your own community and how you take your place in it.**

• To what extent does your church express communal unity in the midst of social diversity?

• Explore your feelings about the level of freedom you enjoy in life. Do you feel free? Or do you feel constrained or oppressed by time, circumstances, social or cultural norms, expectations of others or yourself?

PRAYER CHECK

Turn to "Prayer concerns for this week" in your Study Manual. Review all of your petitions for yourself, intercession for others, joys, and praises. Have there been any reports of God's response? Do you need to remain steadfast and patient with these particular prayers?

CLOSING PRAYER

Dear God, I seek clarity in knowing what it means to be set free by Christ to love those about me. And what about being set free to love me? I want to grasp this new freedom and fill the world with love. I want to give love away as joyously as I receive it from you. Amen.

29 A PASTOR GIVES GUIDANCE

ENCOUNTER THE WORD

Scripture Selection: 1 Timothy 6:3-20

Read the passage, then write down insights you received. Afterward, do the following: 1) Write down the central idea of the passage; 2) Write down the meaning of the passage for today's world; 3) Write down the meaning of the passage for you.

SUMMARY POINTS

— The Pastoral Letters are written as pastoral advice to Timothy and Titus.

— Challenges facing the church include false teachings and church leadership.

— The church is called to live together as a family.

— Here are some characteristics of good leadership: Each leader has a particular function and all functions are equal; and each leader faithfully proclaims, through word and deed, "sound teaching."

— What is important to teach and preach? One God; the call of Christians to be the "household of God"; the desire of God for all to be saved; and sound doctrine.

— Christian leaders are to model godly living so that their sisters and brothers in the household of God can learn to do the same.

CONTEMPLATION AT WEEK'S END

• **What challenges faced the church described in Timothy and Titus? What advice did Paul give?**

• **What challenges confront Christians trying to live together as family in today's world?**

• **We have emphasized throughout this study that, although you are working alone, you do not live in isolation from your family, friends, faith community, or geographic community. List on a sheet of paper all of the ways in which you are responsible to those in your communities.**

PRAYER CHECK

Turn to "Prayer concerns for this week" in your Study Manual. Review all of your petitions for yourself, intercession for others, joys, and praises. Have there been any reports of God's response? Do you need to remain steadfast and patient with these particular prayers?

CLOSING PRAYER

Father, my stewardship is regularly shut down by my frustration that what I can offer is not enough. I forget that whatever amount of service I can give is all that is expected of me and that even a little is helpful to the kingdom. Please prod me when my giving becomes stagnant. Help me train myself always to be observant of community needs and be obedient to your call. Amen.

30 OUR GREAT HIGH PRIEST

ENCOUNTER THE WORD

Scripture Selection: Hebrews 4:14–5:14

Read the passage aloud. Then write down 1) new insights from the Scripture; 2) the central idea of the Scripture; 3) the meaning of the Scripture for today's world; 4) the meaning of the Scripture for you.

SUMMARY POINTS

— Hebrews shows how Jesus is the culmination of the hope of God's people expressed and foreshadowed throughout Scripture.

— Subjected to persecution for their association with Jesus, the believers addressed in Hebrews have begun to doubt that the gifts and promises they have received in Jesus are worth the cost and have begun to slip away from association with the church.

— The writer of Hebrews hopes to correct this perspective, to mobilize the community to help one another persevere in faith and gratitude toward God and Jesus, and to enable a faithful response to each new challenge of discipleship.

CONTEMPLATION AT WEEK'S END

• **What is the message of Hebrews? What does it teach about Christian discipleship?**

• At what points in discipleship do you feel weakest? Do you continue to have faith issues? (Everyone does!) Are you troubled when you do things that Christians are not supposed to do? (There was only one perfect human.) Is your service record thin and unimpressive? (Good goals are never easy to attain.) Call or visit with a faith friend, share your concerns, and frankly ask for encouragement.

PRAYER CHECK

Turn to "Prayer concerns for this week" in your Study Manual. Review all of your petitions for yourself, intercession for others, joys, and praises. Have there been any reports of God's response? Do you need to remain steadfast and patient with these particular prayers?

CLOSING PRAYER

Lord, when I suffer unsteadiness, impatience with myself, and a lack of endurance, remind me that I must not be so bad because, if I were, you and your son would not have sacrificed so dearly for me. Help me love others so much that I am eager to sacrifice for them. Amen.

31 A PEOPLE SET APART

Scripture Selection: 1 Peter 3:8-17

Read the passage aloud. Peter was a rough and often cantankerous fisherman. But he must have mellowed in his later years; because this text is filled with love, sympathy, and compassion. As you read what the passage says about being holy or set apart, try to hear the voice of this gruff old man with his sharp edges worn smooth by the years.

SUMMARY POINTS

— The books of First and Second Peter deliver a particular message for a particular people. These people have been "chosen and destined" for God and are living scattered among strangers. They are "a chosen race, a royal priesthood, a holy nation, God's own people."

— Even in the midst of the trials and tribulations that these people are suffering, God has not abandoned them; they are still God's own people.

— The role of priests in ancient Israel was to serve as intermediaries between God and Israel. They were devoted to reconciling people with God.

— The tribe of the Levites was the only tribe that did not receive territory in the Promised Land. They were scattered among the rest of the tribes of Israel.

— Like the role of the Levite priests, the role of Israel was to be a nation set apart, a kingdom of priests, and a holy nation, to proclaim God's purpose to the nations.

- **For first-century Christians, what did it mean to be a people set apart to proclaim God's purpose to the nations? What does it mean for twenty-first-century Christians?**

- **How do you feel about being called chosen, royal, holy, God's own people?**

- **At what times and in what ways do you feel set apart for the work of the kingdom?**

PRAYER CHECK

Turn to "Prayer concerns for this week" in your Study Manual. Review all of your petitions for yourself, intercession for others, joys, and praises. Have there been any reports of God's response? Do you need to remain steadfast and patient with these particular prayers?

CLOSING PRAYER

Dear God, help me remember that being a member of a chosen race, a royal priesthood, a holy nation, one of God's own people is not a meritorious honor but a blessing with the responsibility to be a blessing to others. Help me always remember my calling. Amen.

32 WE NEVER LOSE HOPE

Scripture Selection: Revelation 21:22–22:5

Read the passage silently, then read it a second time aloud, being alert for sounds, sights, smells, touches, and tastes. Which senses does the Scripture appeal to, and how do you respond? What message of hope comes to you through this passage?

SUMMARY POINTS

— Most scholars regard the Book of Revelation, an apocalyptic writing, as a book of theological insight.

— An apocalypse is an "unveiling" or "revelation" of the true nature of reality.

— Apocalyptic writings were produced during times of severe trial as a way of encouraging believers.

— The message is often conveyed through mysterious images and cryptic language.

— Each of the key apocalyptic concepts—such as the judgment and rebirth of creation—says something important about the character of God, which is the essential subject of apocalyptic literature.

— The conclusion of Revelation describes a reality in which apocalyptic disclosure is unnecessary. God is no longer distant, in heaven and in secret, but is instead on earth, present and known.

— Revelation offers us a theology of creation's completion. No power or principality, no injustice or evil will thwart God's good purpose.

CONTEMPLATION AT WEEK'S END

• **What is the essential subject of apocalyptic writing?**

• **What does it mean to say that the Revelation offers a theology of creation's completion? Does the reality of your faith and life seem like the hidden mystery of the Revelation? Does the meaning of life continue to evade you?**

• **You are nearing the end of a long and deep Bible study. Write on a sheet of paper all of the ways in which your Bible knowledge, personal faith, and relationship with God (and your community and world) have grown. Be hopeful.**

PRAYER CHECK

Turn to "Prayer concerns for this week" in your Study Manual. Review all of your petitions for yourself, intercession for others, joys, and praises. Have there been any reports of God's response? Do you need to remain steadfast and patient with these particular prayers?

CLOSING PRAYER

God of All Creation, in this world that limps along with war, famine, disease, persecution, and environmental degradation, help me not despair but, rather, take hope from peace initiatives, agricultural advancements, medical research triumphs, renewed justice, and ecological protection. Let your people demand and claim the victory. Amen.

33 GIFTS OF EACH DISCIPLE

ENCOUNTER THE WORD

Scripture Selection: Matthew 5:3-12

Read the passage. Your lesson plan was very different this week from all the others. You were not required to read large amounts of Scripture. Your focus was on prayer and what it means to be a disciple. The Beatitudes give a vision of the kingdom. Keep in mind that the Beatitudes are God's blessings as you read them a second time, this time asking yourself how your discipleship can help this vision come true.

SUMMARY POINTS

— God continues to desire our companionship. God's call echoes all the way from Genesis to the Book of the Revelation.

— Not content to be near us, God unbelievably decides to become one of us and one with us in struggle and hope.

— To be truly fulfilled, God's movement toward us in Jesus Christ must be met by a reciprocal movement from our side. This movement toward God involves the following: choosing God's way, receiving God's gifts, doing God's Word, and becoming God's presence.

— By the power of love at work in us, God can do infinitely more than we can ask or even imagine.

CONTEMPLATION AT WEEK'S END

• **What does it mean to become God's presence in the world today? What is your role?**

- **Page 249 of the Study Manual is designed to help groups assess and comment on one another's gifts. For you, this will be a time of self-evaluation. Review all of the pages that you have completed in this week's lesson. What are your gifts for ministry?**

- **Call one or two faith friends and ask them what strengths and gifts they see in you. How can you develop and use your gifts?**

PRAYER CHECK

Turn to "Prayer concerns for this week" in your Study Manual. Review all of your petitions for yourself, intercession for others, joys, and praises. Have there been any reports of God's response? Do you need to remain steadfast and patient with these particular prayers?

CLOSING PRAYER

God, I do not want all of this work I have done in studying your Word to be lodged in my head and not in my heart. Let my heart receive it now. Now that it is in my heart, it cannot be contained. My heart bursts with eagerness to be in ministry. Lord, commission me now to take my revealed gifts out into your world and to be a disciple of Jesus Christ. Amen.

34 A LAST SUPPER TOGETHER

Read through this Covenant Service and enjoy it just as it is; or since you have often been encouraged during this study to call or write to someone about your studies, you might choose to invite someone to come and hear about your study and support you in your discipleship.

TIME OF INDIVIDUAL OR GROUP PRAYER

Scripture and Study Manual (for use by the student alone)

Focus on three words from the Study Manual: *covenant, communion, commitment.*

Think back over your reading of Scripture and the Study Manual to complete this statement: We are covenant people united to Abraham and Sarah, and these are ways we experience that covenant:

Recalling Scripture and the Study Manual, complete this statement: We are new covenant people united to Jesus Christ, and these are ways we experience that new covenant:

As a way of exploring the subject of commitment, identify passages from the Sermon on the Mount as examples of the committed life.

The "Mark of Discipleship" for this lesson is about commitment: Disciples commit their life completely to God to serve as God wills. Describe the differences between the life of commitment and the life of neglect as reflected in "Our Human Condition."

Remember is the theme word for this lesson, and most of the activities focus on remembering. Turn in your Study Manual to page 243 and review the memories you recorded.

ENCOUNTER THE WORD

Scripture Selection: 2 Corinthians 3:2-6.

Read the passage aloud, then paraphrase it. (If you have guests, invite them to also read the Scripture, paraphrase it, and show what they have written.)

SUMMARY POINTS

—The Bible describes a covenant as an agreement between God and God's people.

—The new covenant affirms that "the heart of the problem is the problem of the heart." God thus promises to change the people from the inside out. What God's people cannot do for themselves God will do for them in an act of pure mercy and love.

—Making the new covenant with God is not an individual act. It is a communal one. It is the work of the community of faith.

—The covenant involves not only obligations toward God but also obligations toward the members of the community. So as members of the new covenant community, let us remind ourselves that we can love because we are loved.

COVENANT SERVICE

If you have invited guests, make arrangements ahead of time for those who will have special responsibilities in the covenant service, including arrangements with clergy for Communion. Have hymnals or song sheets available for the songs used in the service. The "Dismissal With Blessing" at the end of the service will bring to a close your study of DISCIPLE.

LOVE FEAST (IF YOU HAVE INVITED GUESTS)

Celebrate the bond among you by sharing time and food together before or after the group meeting.

NOTES

NOTES

NOTES

NOTES

NOTES

NOTES

NOTES

www.ingramcontent.com/pod-product-compliance
Lightning Source LLC
Chambersburg PA
CBHW071103090426
42737CB00013B/2458